Rome

The Piazza del Popolo by night; the obelisk, which dates from the thirteenth century B.C., was brought to Rome from Heliopolis by Augustus.

THIS BEAUTIFUL WORLD VOL. 48

Rome

SEIYŌ KURODA

KODANSHA INTERNATIONAL LTD.
TOKYO, NEW YORK & SAN FRANCISCO

Distributors:
UNITED STATES: *Harper & Row, Publishers, Inc., 10 East 53rd Street, New York, New York 10022.* CANADA: *Fitzhenry & Whiteside Limited, 150 Lesmill Road, Don Mills, Ontario.* CENTRAL AND SOUTH AMERICA: *Feffer & Simons Inc., 31 Union Square, New York, New York 10003.* BRITISH COMMONWEALTH *(excluding Canada and the Far East)*: *TABS, 51 Weymouth Street, London W1N 3LE.* EUROPE: *Boxerbooks Inc., Limmatstrasse 111, 8031 Zurich.* AUSTRALIA AND NEW ZEALAND: *Paul Flesch & Co. Pty. Ltd., 259 Collins Street, Melbourne 3000.* THAILAND: *Central Department Store Ltd., 306 Silom Road, Bangkok.* HONG KONG AND SINGAPORE: *Books for Asia Ltd., 30 Tat Chee Avenue, Kowloon; 65 Crescent Road, Singapore 15.* THE FAR EAST: *Japan Publications Trading Company, P.O. Box 5030, Tokyo International, Tokyo.*

Published by Kodansha International Ltd., 2–12–21 Otowa, Bunkyo-ku, Tokyo 112 and Kodansha International/USA, Ltd., 10 East 53rd Street, New York, New York 10022 and 44 Montgomery Street, San Francisco, California 94104. Copyright © 1974 by Kodansha International Ltd. All rights reserved. Printed in Japan.

LCC 73–89700
ISBN 0–87011–223–6
JBC 0326–784346–2361

First edition, 1974

Contents

First Impressions 7
The Three Ages of Rome 47
Life *alla romana* 79
Map 54

First Impressions

"Thirty-one thousand, two hundred and twenty-eight lire," the man said, handing me what seemed to be gigantic, florid stock certificates. That is virtually my earliest memory of Italy: the size of those enormous bills the Foreign Exchange Bank gave me at the airport, for this was back in the early days before Italy had trimmed its paper currency down to the more customary size, although there are still just as many zeroes in the transaction. Perhaps, had I not been Japanese and accustomed to counting currency in tens of thousands, I might have been even more impressed by the quantity, yet I had exchanged only fifty dollars.

It was a beautiful day. The sky was clean and clear and the smell of the sea hung in the air. I had no idea Rome lay so near the water, but less than half an hour ago we had been flying over the clear blue Mediterranean, and just a few minutes before landing we crossed crowded, beige-colored beaches. My ignorance, when I thought about it, rather embarrassed me. In fact, I could feel myself blushing, for my prior concept of Rome had not extended beyond two very distant images difficult to reconcile: haughty, toga-clad senators in vast marble halls and spaghetti-eating, wine-drinking, always laughing carousers at sidewalk cafes. There was a great deal for me to learn.

That first short stay, only three days, back in 1963 eventually proved to be the antipasto of a great and glorious feast that I am still devouring; but at the time I had no inkling of what was to come. It took a while for me and Rome to reach that pleasant state of intimacy we now enjoy.

Had I visited Rome with the great expectations so many visitors have when they come for the first time to this city whose name, after all, is the source of the word "romance," I am sure my first impressions would have been quite different. On that trip in from the airport, I would have taken in the weathered stone farmhouses, the shawled women dressed in black, working small fields that did not look very fertile, and the first glimpses of the meandering Tiber, tamed and peaceful between high banks. I would have tried to make out those seven famous hills, long since camouflaged by countless generations of builders. What I do remember is suddenly being confronted and overwhelmed by the Colosseum, breathtaking in its form and presence. And then all too soon it was gone, and we were in that maze of streets, wide and narrow and even then choked with traffic, that constitutes present-day Rome.

My next recollection is an unexpected awareness of the excitement and the tension of the journey seeping from me as the hotel elevator clanged shut. Some years later, as a similar sound re-evoked that strange impression, I recalled it with surprise, for I had studied Roman history by then and, that later time, was reflecting on one of history's footnotes. Since its first, and almost total, destruction early in the fourth century B.C., Rome's vicissitudes have been many, and virtually the only ancient building that is almost perfectly preserved is the Pantheon—behind whose marble veneer lies concrete. Although they did not invent it, the Romans, beginning around the second century B.C., were the first to use concrete extensively in construction. The last Roman emperor of the West was deposed in A.D. 476; in the next century the city was for a time all but deserted; and concrete fell into disuse until the late eighteenth century.

This is one of the strange facts about the fabulous city that I eventually learned; but on my first visit, as I stepped into the wrought-iron cage of the elevator, its shaft encircled by the staircase, I was a long way from reflecting upon the uses of concrete in ancient Roman construction. Now time almost seemed to stop, the door slowly rumbled closed, and, with a great whirring that seemed to emanate from distant medieval foundations, the cage started, very gently, upward. It was a delightful sensation, and when I thought about it in later years, I remembered it thankfully, for all the cares of the journey seemed suddenly to disappear, melting away my apprehensions.

Nevertheless, I found those first three days rather lonely. And it was all, I freely admit, my own fault, for Italians are really among the easiest people in the world to know, at least superficially. The harsh, bustling world of today has changed everyone a bit, and Italians, alas, are no exception. But even then they struck me as an extraordinarily cheerful people, smiling and singing from breakfast to the time when the porter, finally and gracefully, swept away the ghostly footprints of the last late-night reveler. Smiling and cheerful, yes; but almost none of them seemed to speak English. And I spoke no Italian whatsoever.

Perhaps I was unlucky in my choice of a hotel, but I soon discovered that the only member of that cheerful, friendly, vocal staff who spoke any English was the manager, and he was far too busy a man to spend several hours a day answering my numerous and very naive questions. So I spent my time, that first brief visit, wandering the streets of Rome, a solitary explorer too shy to accost strangers—although I know now that they would have been happy and eager to help me, and that many of them spoke quite enough English for us to communicate.

So for three almost wordless days (and it should be noted that we Japanese do like to talk) I visited the great sights, sights which produced a jumble that only years later began to make etchings on the *tabula rasa*. I wandered from one end of Rome to another, to ancient Rome, to Renaissance Rome, to modern Rome; I visited the famous squares, the great basilicas, the antique remains, the Renaissance palaces towering over narrow streets and wide piazzas; but strangely enough the only monument I recall with any clarity from those first ramblings was one that no true lover of Rome loves very well. I am almost embarrassed to say that it was that white marble colossus (some folk use less kindly words), the Victor Emmanuel Monument.

It is quite clear that I was far from being, that first visit, a Rome-lover—or even a Rome-appreciator. Yet I think it is not surprising that the monument should make a startling first impression—not for its beauty, since it is far from possessing that quality (an elusive quality that many other Roman constructions possess in abundance), but for its sheer bulk, its glittering white marble, and its very presence. It is *there*. It does indeed bestride Rome like a colossus. If it is true that all roads lead to Rome, then surely all roads in Rome lead to this man-made pinnacle, Rome's eighth hill and a symbol of modern Italy, that united country which evolved with Garibaldi and which was no longer a mere geographical expression. But I shall have more to say about that later.

And I shall have more to say, too, about happy Roman evenings. On my first visit, after night fell, I would tuck myself into a corner of some rowdy cafe, listening to the music of Italy, envying the groups of people at crowded, noisy tables, and fervently praying for a gift for languages. My prayer was not granted.

Two years slipped by before I did what all visitors to Rome are supposed to do: return. This, too, was a short stay of only three days, but it was much happier and more rewarding, and that for at least two reasons. One was the weather. I had come to Rome the first time in the dread month of August, the peak of the Italian summer, when the sun is relentless and the dusty, scorching sirocco blows up from North Africa. During mid-August (Ferragosto), all self-respecting Romans escape to the mountains or the beaches or somewhere, *anywhere* but Rome, leaving their city to those who cannot escape, to the tourists, and to the guides who shepherd the sweltering tourists to the cool fountains and high halls of the old buildings.

This second visit of mine was in October, the famous *ottobrata romana* universally acknowledged to be Rome's best month. The air had already turned a bit cool, the winds were soft, and I could walk the streets of the city in comfort. And that brings me to my second reason, for I now had a guide too, a Japanese friend who lived in Rome and worked for Japan Airlines. He took me in hand and helped me unravel the sights of the city. He told me some of the stories and bits of gossip that bring those sights to life for the visitor. He freed me—I am happy to report—from the magnetic white pull of the Victor Emmanuel Monument.

And he introduced me, properly and formally, to the secrets of true Italian cooking. It was the seed of a love affair that will, I hope, go on bearing fruit for a long time to come. And my friend also took me to a few of Rome's many nightclubs, places at which I had earlier gazed longingly from the sidewalk as if they were forbidden temples. I will not say I was disappointed when I finally got inside them, for vivacious Italian girls make fine dancing partners, but as with nightclubs all over the world reality tempers the frolics of the imagination.

It was not, however, until my third visit to Rome that I began to feel truly close to the city that was destined to become for me a second home, a home from home. Quite obviously it had never gripped me strongly before, for during these years I had been flying all over the world on photographic assignments and was often in Europe. So I could easily have gone more frequently to Rome and spent more time there. Instead, when I could I preferred to escape to the Swiss mountains.

Some cities, like people, need to be known very well before they can be loved, and maybe Rome is one of these. Venice is not —you either love it or you hate it at first sight, and I think perhaps the same is true of a few other great cities. But as Rome, an ancient and a modern capital, with layer upon layer of life behind it, welcomes the tourist, it also confuses and bewilders him. There is simply too much, covering too long a span, from the ruins in the Archeological Museum to the relics who frequent the outdoor cafes of the Via Veneto. Rome, as I say, is a city that needs knowing.

It was in April 1969, on a flight to Italy, that I happened to become friendly with a fellow passenger, and he chanced to be not only an Italian but a true Roman, *un vero romano*, one born and brought up in the city. Happily he also happened to be a friendly, knowledgeable, gregarious fellow who spoke fluent English; and it was he, more than anyone, who colored the nature of my future relationship with that (one can only hope) eternal city.

One day, as we were coming out of the Vatican museum, he mentioned casually that he had another Japanese friend—a young man who had come to Rome with his wife to study art. At this I grew quite excited, for we Japanese (everyone, I think, agrees) are a parochial people: we enjoy nothing so much as the company of our fellow countrymen.

"Can I meet them?" I cried.

"Well, of course," said my Italian friend, with some surprise. "Why on earth not?"

We hailed a taxi and in ten minutes reached the narrow Trastevere street where the Japanese art student lived with his wife and daughter. They welcomed us graciously, and soon we were all sitting around drinking an aperitif and comparing life in Italy with our own Japan. They too spoke English as well as fluent Italian, and both husband and wife agreed that they felt utterly at home here and hoped to stay on quite a while longer. At this I began to wonder why *I* had not felt at home here, and after a moment I heard myself say, "I'd like to stay on here for a while, too."

This happy Japanese family, it turned out, had a guest room, and after we had talked a bit longer they shyly offered it to me for my stay in Rome. I accepted with alacrity, moved in the next day (mine was the best room in the house, by the way, and made me feel a little guilty), and here I finally learned to love Rome, her people and her monuments, in all their aspects, both splendid and humdrum.

Venturing out each morning into Roman traffic is a nerve-wracking start to any day. Minute Fiats zip through the narrow streets, often scraping the curb, and seem almost to dive through the legs of pedestrians. To compound the hazard, many narrow Roman streets (like many narrow Japanese streets) lack proper sidewalks, so the pedestrian not only has to cope with those darting Fiats that seem to be everywhere, he has to cope with them on their own ground. It can be a more than harrowing experience. Everything, indeed, is like a speeded-up Keystone Cops comedy, with collision a mere hair's breadth away. Even the frenzied streets of Tokyo seem fairly calm in comparison.

By 7:30 in the morning city noises are deafening. Motorcars their engines screaming, whinny to a stop before the frantic whistles of the policemen and then rev their motors to a high-pitched shriek in their eagerness to be the first away. The poor bemused sightseer is best advised to scamper off to the top of a nearby monument and wait until the activity diminishes a bit and the noise abates a few decibels in volume. And with this new perspective comes the feeling that he is opting out, retreating into history while present-day Romans live, as their ancestors did, at the center of the world.

Nevertheless, it was during such early morning walks, when I used to help with the family shopping, adding my *buon giorno* to the constant chorus of others, that I began to feel part of the city and my heart began to open to it. Strangely, though, or perhaps not so strangely, for I always find it difficult to analyze and isolate the growth and shaping of my own feelings, it was the south of Italy that won my affection first. Rome had to wait her turn; then she pounced with a vengeance.

As that is a picture-book about Rome, I shall make no attempt to describe my trip into the south—to Naples and still enchanting if slightly soiled Capri, to the other islands of Ischia and Procida, to the staggering ruins of Pompeii and Herculaneum, to Sorrento and Positano and Amalfi, to some of the fairest towns and loveliest countryside in all Italy—save to note that for some reason my sojourn there served as a kind of catalyst. The whole time I was in a state of perpetual excitement; indeed, I could hardly sleep remembering the extraordinary sights and sensations of the day and the thought of new ones on the morrow. My shutter finger grew completely irrepressible, and wherever I pointed my lens there was a picture, framed and perfect. For a photographer, this was truly paradise—and when after a time I returned to Rome, I returned a somehow changed man. That very evening, as golden dusk fell upon Michelangelo's great dome of St. Peter's and as I stood there watching the gorgeous spectacle, I made a resolution: I would come to live in Rome. The next day, as though to seal the compact, I told my Japanese friends about my resolution—which, I hardly need say, they vociferously approved. And before the year was out, my resolution had become reality.

It was the last week in December when my wife and I with our two daughters, both of them bubbling over with excitement, boarded a plane at Tokyo airport and headed toward the pole, to descend on Rome from the north, like the barbarians fifteen hundred years before us. And it was the day before Christmas when we arrived in Rome. By that time our daughters' excitement had communicated itself to us more staid elders, and our whole little Japanese family was virtually quivering with anticipation as we entered the famous city.

We grudgingly took a little time to unpack and wash before scurrying out into the streets. Despite the strong winds blowing down from the northeast and the scudding clouds that threatened winter rain or snow, I knew that Christmas Eve would be a perfect moment to look for the first time at the city which, once it had discarded its pagan gods, became the center of Western Christendom. For many hundreds of millions, of course, it still is, and even Italians who seldom go to church will celebrate Christmas with a gusto and verve and enthusiasm that we found both astonishing and contagious. We Japanese celebrate Christmas too, but for that vast majority of us who are not Christians it is little more than a secular holiday imported from the West, a good excuse to carouse and exchange presents—both of them old and deeply ingrained Japanese habits.

I had been told that many Italians, perhaps because of their intimacy with the Church, tend to be a bit cynical about it, but we felt no hint of that as we watched the long lines of people, with flickering candles in their hands, that wound solemnly through the darkened streets toward the great basilicas, where midnight mass was to be triumphantly celebrated.

Although I can hardly qualify as an authority on the subject, I tried to explain to my children that these huge and ancient churches which they regarded with pop-eyed wonder were not cathedrals but rather basilicas—that is, churches built in the antique Roman style, perhaps making use of antique Roman material, and granted the papal right to call themselves basilicas. St. John Lateran is the one and only cathedral of Rome, the seat of her bishop and so, in a sense, the cathedral of the Catholic world.

Even St. Peter's is only a basilica, and the same is true of Santa Maria Maggiore, where we were going first because it is not only a church of great beauty and distinction but also a favorite on Christmas Eve with the people of Rome. In fact, it was here that, in older days, the popes celebrated the first Christmas Eve mass. For one thing, the basilica was built—so legend has it—at the express order of the Virgin herself, who appeared, one August night in the fourth century, before Pope Liberius and commanded him to erect a church on the spot where he would find snow falling the following August day. This—again according to legend—he did, though according to historians Santa Maria Maggiore was not built until the following century and under the aegis of another pope, Sixtus III.

In any case, it has for many centuries been intimately associated with the virgin birth, and among its famous relics there is what purports to be a bit of the holy crib in which the infant Jesus slept. This Christmas Eve it was already crowded when we entered, although we had come quite early. The children gasped at the splendor of the flickering lights reflected on the lovely golden Renaissance ceiling, on the rows of very fine classical columns that line the nave, and on the brilliant mosaics with their golden tiles. It was a sight that nothing in their lives in Japan had prepared them for. We waited until after the solemn procession in which the reliquary of the holy crib is carried around the church, and even then I could hardly induce them to come away, but I wanted them to see the Vatican too in all its Christmas Eve glory. Although we were late, the streets around St. Peter's were still jammed with people, and we could still hear the echoes of the carols that are sung in the great church and that resound not only in the colonnaded square outside but also across the Tiber to the city and the world.

A week later all solemnity is forgotten, and the New Year is welcomed in to a blaze and furor of thousands of fireworks. Rockets explode in every corner of the sky to illuminate the night and transform it into a vast fiery furnace. The agitation in the heavens is reflected below in the exuberant frenzy of the Roman people, who with demoniac yells hurtle fireworks and—when those run out—just plain empty bottles into the air. On this day, shortly before nightfall, the myriads of parked cars that customarily litter the streets mysteriously vanish; all garages are full to bursting, and cramped courtyards behind locked gates become harbors to shelter precious family vehicles from rampaging mobs. For one brief night the streets of Rome are the sole province of pedestrians.

My family was as astonished by New Year as it had been by Christmas—and for quite a different reason. In Japan, as I have noted, Christmas tends to be a secular and rather boisterous occasion, while the welcoming of the New Year is a family affair, quiet and sedate. Most people, if they leave home at all, go no further than to a neighboring Shinto shrine, so it was especially startling for the children to see this Roman extravaganza when the citizens fling off the pent-up frustrations of the year that has just ended to start a new year fresh.

Indeed, from the children's point of view, we could hardly have arrived in Rome at a better time, for it was also the season of

Befana, the gruff old witch who substitutes for the more northerly Santa Claus and who reaches her day of glory on January 6, the Epiphany. Her dwelling-place is the Piazza Navona, one of Rome's largest and most splendid squares, where early in December booths start going up that eventually, in their hundreds, will offer for sale just about anything and everything, although it is chiefly children who are catered to. Of course there are all the figures that one might want to decorate a Christmas crib with, but there is a great deal else besides; toys of every description, noisemakers, space suits, the mini-machinery of war, monster masks and costumes, colored balloons stretching into the sky, cotton candy and finger-sticking toffee. Social historians tell us that the effigies of the three wise men and the other traditional crèche characters actually have their origin in the terra-cotta statuettes that were sold at a similar fair held in a similar place to celebrate Rome's ancient pagan Saturnalia; but this is not a matter that in any way affects or dampens the ardor of the thousands upon thousands of screaming children who come to the Piazza Navona from all parts of Rome as well as from the surrounding countryside and who, with their more mature escorts, throng the square both day and night.

Piazza Navona itself is a fascinating square with an equally fascinating history. It is long and narrow, the shape of Domitian's stadium, over which it was built. The stadium, the Circus Agonalis, is said to have given its present-day name to the Piazza, for in the course of time Agonalis became N'Agona and that finally became Navona. True? Who knows? What certainly is true is that two thousand years ago chariots were whipped around the track, in the center of which now stands Bernini's great Fountain of the Rivers, decorated with four monumental statues representing the Nile, the Ganges, the Danube, and the Río de la Plata. What certainly is also true (at least when we were there) is that many a modern-day taxi driver, taking advantage of a clear stretch and seeking to emulate his forefathers, will whip his twenty horses into a tire-screeching lather. That no doubt is why, even then, there was talk of closing the Piazza Navona to wheeled traffic.

Almost continuously throughout its life Domitian's Circus has been the site of spectacles. As recently as the mid-fifteenth century it remained virtually unchanged and was used for knightly jousting. And even after it was remade and its three fountains erected, it continued to play that particular role in the life of Rome. Indeed, until just a century ago, it was the stage for a bizarre summer festival, when the drainpipes for the fountains were blocked and water overflowed into the square. Then it was fashionable to decorate one's carriage and drive around the piazza, stopping off at one or another of the gay parties taking place along the brink. Quite evidently, *la dolce vita* is not a recent innovation in Rome.

The Roman calendar is far too full to be described here in detail, but it would be highly improper not to say a word about the city's chief and most solemn feast, that denominated in the Christian world as Holy Week. It begins and ends, as indeed it should, at the basilica of St. Peter's, but throughout the week all Rome takes part and plays a role.

On Palm Sunday people throng into St. Peter's Square, Bernini's overwhelmingly impressive masterpiece, bearing palm leaves to be blessed. Then, in the days that follow, there are processions all over the city, special ceremonies in the Catacombs and the Colosseum, and incredibly beautiful music in many of the churches and chapels. Tenebrae, of course, is particularly moving when, in late afternoon, the altar candles are extinguished one by one until at the end of the service the church is in darkness, the singing ceases, and the people leave in silence.

Good Friday, naturally, is a very solemn day. It is the day when many Romans go to Santa Croce in Gerusalemme to join in the procession and to pray, if they can, at the chapel of St. Helena, the mother of Constantine, who is credited with discovering the True Cross. And many Romans go to nearby Scala Santa, which legend identifies with the stairway that Jesus climbed in the palace of Pontius Pilate but that history says could not possibly be. In any case, more people go there than the stairway can accommodate, and those who are fortunate enough to gain admittance ascend the steps on their knees.

On Holy Saturday, there is the splendid ceremony of the kindling of the sacred flame in the basilicas as well as in the simpler and more ancient churches; and then, the following day, there comes the climax, the moment that many Romans have waited for and many visitors to Rome have come for—the appearance before the city and the world of the Pope to give his Easter blessing.

We did our best to see as much of what Rome offers as we could while we were there, but I knew that a lifetime would not suffice to see it all. And for the stranger, getting around in the city can sometimes attain the proportions of a nightmare. Romans are almost inevitably charming, but they often tend to grow a trifle impatient with people who pretend they cannot understand Italian. Many Italians expect everyone to understand their language; this they imply with a generous gesture of an extended palm, raising their eyebrows at the obviousness of the fact. And it so often took us quite a bit longer to find the sight or the restaurant we were seeking than it should have; and sometimes we never found it at all. An unescorted and attractive girl, it should be noted, has no such problem; suddenly there seems to exist a common language, even if it means disgorging scorned bits of academic force-fed English.

After we had resigned ourselves to the fact that sometimes there is a language problem, we decided that the best answer to traveling long distances inside the city was the bus. For a time I rented a car but even though I had been tested in Tokyo traffic, I crumpled before that of Rome. Horse-drawn carriages still exist, and of course they are fun for a time, like the gondolas of Venice, but they are slow and they are also likely to be quite expensive. Rome's electric trams are fast disappearing from the center, and Rome's subway is not yet of much use.

So there remains the bus; and as with most European cities, especially in the hotter climes, life on a bus has a style all its own. Faced with the temporary intimacy a crowded bus necessitates, northern peoples tend to draw in on themselves while southerners become expansive. Romans display the latter talent to the full. Apart from the quietest time of day—early afternoon, when most of the people who are still awake and abroad are tourists—the Roman bus is likely to be bursting at the seams, with nearly everyone standing and the driver guiding his bus as if there were no tomorrow. Nevertheless, we found we never missed our stop, for we had only to mumble the word and we would be seen off by our fellow travelers with as much ceremony and friendly goodwill as if we were leaving Naples in a transatlantic liner. Often there would even be a chorus of "goodbyes"—for English is not really all *that* bad. It's just that no one likes to have it sprung on him.

Two weeks after I arrived with my family, some Japanese friends came for their Roman holiday and I, though still a comparative stranger myself, found I was to be their guide. They were stopping at a small hotel in the center that I was unfamiliar with, but intrepidly I poked the hood of my little car out of the garage and in a moment I was swept away in a flood of traffic, only to be caught time and again in narrow one-way streets which, like little eddies in a stream, kept luring me off in directions I did not want to go, where I would find myself led in an endless circle with no apparent escape. If I tried to stop the car for a moment to consult my map of the city, a raucous chorus of horns would force me forward again into the maelstrom.

Eventually I found an inch of space in one of the old squares (now, alas, used as parking lots) and there I left my car. After only a few minutes' wait I was lucky enough to flag down a taxi, the driver of which knew, of course, exactly how to get to the hotel I had been vainly trying to reach for nearly an hour. It was, I am embarrassed to relate, only a few minutes away. Shortly after that humiliating experience I turned in the car, and for the rest of our Roman visit we used buses—or that even more dependable means of transportation, shank's mare.

1. The Milvian Bridge stands at the site of Constantine's victory over Maxentius in the fourth century, one of history's most important battles.

3–4. Piazza di Spagna has for some three centuries been the tourist heart of Rome. *Right*, the Barcaccia, the famous fountain in the center, designed by Bernini. *Overleaf*, a view of the square at dusk, with the fashionable shopping street, Via Condotti, leading off into the distance.

2. View from the Pincian Hill, with the dome of St. Peter's dominating the far distance.

7. Piazza del Quirinale (*opposite*), with the obelisk and the colossal Roman statues (probably copies of Greek originals), sometimes known as "Castor and Pollux," sometimes as "The Horsetamers."

5–6. Fountains of Rome: *below*, Bernini's celebrated Triton fountain in Piazza Barberini; and *right*, the Trevi fountain, into which visitors to Rome toss coins to ensure a return.

10. Victor Emmanuel Monument (*overleaf*), another major landmark, commemorates the unification of Italy under her first king.

9. Eighteenth-century facade (*right*) of St. John Lateran, cathedral of Rome. With its colossal statue of Jesus flanked by saints and doctors of the Church, it is one of the landmarks of Rome.

8. A first communion at Santa Maria Maggiore, one of the seven basilicas.

11–12. Piazza Navona, Rome's handsomest square, is largely a seventeenth-century construction on the site of the ancient stadium of Domitian. The fountain (*below*) is one of three in which Bernini is said to have had a hand and which help make the square such a pleasant place to wander through and relax in.

◁ 13. Ponte S. Angelo (*see preceding page*) as viewed from the height of Castel S. Angelo.

14–17. Roman scenes: flower-sellers (*right*) stand at almost every street-corner; street-corners (*below*) also serve other purposes; the great walls of Rome (*below right*) are remarkably well preserved; Rome's many fountains (*opposite*) provide cool, drinkable water on hot, thirsty days.

18–19. A large part of the Vatican, the world's smallest state, consists of cool, relaxing gardens. In the background (*right*) towers the great dome of St. Peter's.

20–23. Vatican museums are inexhaustible treasure-houses. *Right*, one of the main corridors; *opposite*, a handsome spiral stairway; *below*, the Apollo Belvedere and the Laocoon.

24–26. Mussolini's grand international exposition (E.U.R.) was never held, but its buildings now provide spacious suburban living quarters and also house museums, sports events, exhibitions and conferences. Some structures (*right and overleaf*) are futuristic in design, while others (*below*) echo the styles of the ancient Romans embodied in such monuments as the Colosseum.

The Three Ages of Rome

There are three Romes, each superimposed on the other. The modest beginnings of the Eternal City are traced back to shepherds and swineherds who settled around the Palatine Hill during the eighth century B.C. and built up, as best they could, a fortress town to withstand the expansion of the Etruscans from the north. The Romans themselves are very clear about the foundations of their city. It was established in 753 B.C. by Romulus, the son of Rhea Silvia, a virgin servant of the Gods. He was abandoned with his twin brother Remus to be later rescued from their raft on the flooded Tiber by a she-wolf.

The Republic was formed in 510 B.C., when legend and myth give way to history—though the amazing progress of the Republic is far more worthy of legend. The Republic in turn gave way to the grandeur of the Empire and Rome's finest hour.

Structurally the second Rome began during the Renaissance when Rome was ruled by the Pope. Much of the present-day splendor, most of what we think of as Rome in our idle dreams in some backwater of civilization, is the Rome that was built during the sixteenth, seventeenth and eighteenth centuries by architects such as Michelangelo, Borromini and the great master of the Baroque, Gian Lorenzo Bernini (1598–1680).

Finally, after the reunification of Italy in 1870, Rome—the

natural capital of the new state—entered its third and most unfortunate phase as a modern city. To explore Rome is to search out beneath the blanket of modernity the beauty which still abounds. Often it is obvious, proud and resplendent, laughing down the cascade of a Bernini fountain, but it may be serene, as the sculptures on a Borromini church, or even hidden behind some modern facade that is oblivious of the treasures it conceals.

But let us begin our tour of Rome from the top of the Capitoline Hill in the Piazza del Campidoglio. It is not a particularly high or imposing rise but, along with its twin, the Palatine Hill, it can be considered the ancient center of Rome. Although surrounded by the rowdy chaos of an all-too-active city, the square is as peaceful as it was when first conceived and built by Michelangelo. It was he who designed the two palaces to the right and the left of the Senatorial Palace and which are now museums of ancient sculpture. It was he, too, who created the magnificent flights of steps which curve on either side of this palace. And it was he who brought the mounted statue of Marcus Aurelius, already well over a thousand years old, and centered it in the mosaic of the Piazza. It is the only complete example of Roman equestrian sculpture dating from the Imperial era. An old story has it that the statue was formerly of gold and is now covered with a patina. As soon as the patina wears away or otherwise disappears and the gold is revealed, Rome, and hence the world, will come to an end.

The Senatorial Palace is now the Town Hall, which is quite appropriate, for it is built on the same site as the Tabularium which served a similar function when it was constructed two thousand years earlier. Here, the laws, carved on bronze tablets, were kept and used to settle the squabbles of the Forum.

Six centuries before Christ, this hill was also the site of the Temple of Jupiter. And it is here that the victorious Caesars, dressed in flowing gowns with vermilion faces and riding milk white horses, came from battle to do homage. From a terrace outside the temple, known as the Tarpeian Rock, traitors were thrown to their deaths before the crowds of the Forum. According to legend, the first to suffer such punishment was Tarpeia, a young girl who unlocked the Rock's gate to admit the enemy Sabines.

Every step up the marble staircase to the Capitoline Hill presents a memorial to history. And the reverence we feel as we climb up can only be an echo of the way those women felt so many years ago as they climbed these steps on their knees to request of Juno a husband, a child, or even domestic peace.

Today pieces of history are still being found among the foundations of the ancient buildings that are now surrounded by newer ones, themselves three hundred years old.

Before descending, after spending all of a long morning on the Hill instead of the brief half hour we had allotted, there is still time, expandable Italian time, to enter the cool nave of the Church of Santa Maria in Aracoeli, built on the site where the sybil Tiburtina told Augustus of the advent of Christ. For much of the Middle Ages this was considered the center of the religious and even the social life of Rome. As control of the Church wavered between one faction and the next, episcopal debate rang loud and long as the famous and fashionable attempted to solve the problems of the world. At Christmastime the Child of Aracoeli, an image of the infant Jesus, is put in the crib which the sick and the troubled visit, praying for a miracle.

Nearby, considered the focal point of Rome, is the Piazza Venezia, perhaps my favorite square—if only because it is from here that I can orient myself and so feel least bewildered—and it is here that I have taken some of my best photographs. It is dominated not by the Capitoline Hill nor by the severely styled

Palazzo Venezia, but by that great neo-classical wedding cake of a memorial to King Victor Emmanuel II, the Vittoriano, constructed over a period of twenty-one years to celebrate the fiftieth anniversary of the Kingdom of Italy. It is the Altar of the Fatherland and the Tomb of the Unknown Warrior. There are allegories of the triumph of Patriotism and Labor, statues of Right, Sacrifice, Concord and Strength, and high in the clouds are two chariots, each with four horses in harness, representing Liberty and Unity.

But let us circumnavigate the Vittoriano along the Via dei Fori Imperiali until we arrive at the entrance to the Roman Forum. For a long time this was the only forum, but after the city grew and it was found too small to cope with the increasing number of voluble citizens, others were built. It was also the largest and is now the best preserved. The site of the Roman Forum was originally an unhealthy marshland in the midst of settlements. It was chosen by the inhabitants of the surrounding hills as a meeting place for trade. Later, markets and temples were built, and eventually it became the focus of political and administrative activities as well.

It seems so small at first, this famous Forum. It is hard to imagine great affairs of state being decided in these cramped surroundings. But after wandering awhile among the scattered stones, the broken steps, the truncated pillars, gradually the Forum emerges complete in the mind's eye. For each single traveler, alone with his imagination, standing on the now grass-covered cobbles of the Via Sacra, the Sacred Way, once again the Forum lives. First comes the noise. The chorus of market shouts from the farmers in from the country with their chickens, flour and fruit. And the artisans crying their wares, clay pots, Etruscan vases and rough parchment—all the loud but mellifluous sounds of an Italian market.

But the tradesmen's sounds fade away as, upon the Rostrum (now only the stone foundation, but once faced with marble) the white-clad senators gather: their faces firm and proud, short wiry hair—blond in my imagination thanks to the color of the stone in which their images have reached us—and standing in perpetual profile to show to good advantage those all-knowing noses.

Here once grew the yeast which was to ferment throughout the states of the Western world. Here, on this patch of land, bruised since by barbarians and ignorant sons, Western civilization spent much of its adolescence. Arrogant, optimistic and ambitious, it had a strength which we can still feel clearly.

Today, the two arches at either end—the Arch of Septimius Severus and the more famous Arch of Titus—are in the best state of preservation. Both were erected to celebrate victories in battle. Is it not ironical, I wonder, that these should have been built more sturdily than the Basilica and Temples where the steps now lead to bare foundations as though long since stripped of their aspirations? But the Curia, the Senate House, still stands, and it is good that it has survived, for it was the birthplace of Roman Law, the beginning of a system which, to a greater or lesser extent, must have affected every country in the world.

Here was the start of parliamentary law which, only a hundred years ago, reached out as far as my native Japan, and is still adding converts to its cause. Perhaps in those days there was less pressure, fewer lobbyists to pacify, but the conduct of this first senate seems to have surpassed its successors.

We cannot leave the Forum without a quiet saunter among the ruins of the Temple of the Vestal Virgins. Throughout the greater part of Rome's glory this temple, now just a few brick walls, housed the sacred flame, tended with love by six vestal virgins who, though the most revered women in Rome, were under threat of dire torture if the flame was allowed to go out.

Rubbing sticks together to start a fire was no easier before the properties of phosphorous were discovered than it is now, and in primitive societies it was customary to keep a fire perpetually burning from which new ones could be taken. This fire often took on religious significance and such was the case in Rome. Fire, far from being the stuff that later hells were made of, was a symbol of purity, a symbol to be guarded by the unsullied. And so the virgins were chosen.

Across from the Senate Building the Temple of Saturn is silhouetted against the afternoon sun. First built almost 2500 years ago, its eight pillars rise high to a great pediment, but behind this magnificent portico is air, silence, sky. The romantic and enthusiastic who come to Rome see, behind that entrance, the excitement and history of Rome.

Beyond the Forum is that landmark which, through the aegis of tourist agencies, has become synonymous with Rome, the Colosseum. It is as awe-inspiring in reality as it seems in photographs. Although it was used as a stone quarry by every builder in the neighborhood for hundreds of years, it is still remarkably preserved. Though the finer ornamentation has long since disappeared it is still amazing in its complexity and is structurally complete.

Its four-storied exterior wall is over fifty meters high. The first three stories have arches divided by columns—Doric on the first floor, then Ionic and lastly Corinthian. These columns are not load-bearing and so have survived surprisingly well. When the Colosseum was first built, in each arch on the second and third stories was a statue. More amazing still is the fact that it was built on a marsh, with its foundations set in water.

With the Emperor and Court, the mysterious Vestal Virgins, and a crowd of 50,000 attending, it must have been a wonderful sight. The lowest range of seats was reserved for army officers, the next for the citizens, and the upper for the people. A day at the Games was occasion for great pageantry and splendor. Yet what went on in the arena was as barbaric as the city was civilized, and the wonderful sight of the overflowing, pulsating arena must have struck terror into many a criminal or Christian destined to die in its dirt.

In the morning came the animals—lions, elephants, hippopotamuses and other exotica from the far-flung corners of the Empire. They were captured, caged and brought to Rome for combat and slaughter. Their opponents were *bestiarii* who fought them with nets, spears and other more fanciful weapons. The animals were brought up from the subterranean passages beneath the arena by pulleys and windlasses; there was little chance they would return.

But these fights were only preliminaries. Like the *maku-uchi* bouts of a Japanese sumo-wrestling tournament, they often attracted only the totally dedicated fans and the plebeians. The real battles began in the afternoon with the gladiators.

First came the grand parade. The gladiators marched around the arena before lining up to greet the Emperor: "Hail Caesar. We who are about to die salute you!" It was no idle cry. In contests the defeated gladiator had the right to appeal to the crowd for his life; thumbs up meant life, down, death. But not all contestants had that chance. Sometimes a company of gladiators fought until only one survived. Fellow gladiators who had lived and trained together had to turn upon their comrades in a final fight of survival. Criminals sentenced to death were also expected to kill each other in gory battles. The Christians were usually pitted against animals.

As the sun set, a spectre would appear, mallet in hand, searching among the blood and gore and tapping the heads of the fallen to discover those not yet dead.

South of the Colosseum one can make a lonely pilgrimage to the Palatine Hill at the opposite end of the Forum from the Capitoline Hill. There is little to see now on the mound where Rome began and from which the word "palace" originated, though the House of Livia still exists. Livia was the second wife of Augustus, survived him, after causing havoc with his ancestors, and succeeded to the throne jointly with her son.

North of the Piazza Venezia is the Rome of the Renaissance. The main avenue, Via del Corso, bursts with traffic and impetuous citizens trying to rebuild Rome in half a day and tourists, packaged and air-conditioned in growling buses or running into banks to prepare for another round. It is hard to imagine what architectural gems lie, serenely, just out of range of the policeman's commanding whistle. The Gods of Rome are laughing. They laugh alike at the perplexed foreigner and the native whose priorities are disturbed.

Just to the east of the Corso, among the dark narrow alleys, stone churches, closed shutters and beaded curtained bars selling wine and Coca-Cola, almost unnoticed at first behind a string of parked cars, is the Trevi Fountain. Rather than a grandiose carving dominating in size, strength or beauty the surrounding streets, it is like a floodlit stage where some youthful drama is enacted. The sculptures, like the water, emerge full of vitality from the rock. Horses, eager for life, mingle with the water playing on yellow rocks and cascading into the pool. Facing south, it is in constant sunlight and contrasts with the shadowed lanes.

And everyone must wish, their back turned to the fountain. The first coin tossed is said to mean that you will return to Rome. After that stories diverge, but the cost of wishes withstands inflation and three is still a bargain. In some weeks as much as two or three hundred dollars is collected from the fountain and distributed to charity.

Back on the Corso at Piazza Colonna is the column of Marcus Aurelius which was erected in A.D. 176 to commemorate a victory over the Germans. A complex frieze spirals to the top, thirty meters high. The bottom part represents some detail of the war but the rest is lost unless you bring binoculars.

Farther along the Corso, a left turn at the Via Condotti soon separates the conscientious historian from the dilettante. This is the Bond Street of Rome. Behind unpretentious fronts are the fashion houses which bring the rich and famous flocking to Rome to mince and pirouette in cloistered salons. So why not saunter, window-shopping and dreaming? Or are the sight of the Spanish Steps and the Piazza di Spagna drawing you like a magnet toward the end of the street?

In the center of the Piazza di Spagna is a strange fountain, shaped like a sinking boat. It is called La Barcaccia ("The Old Tub") and was designed by the elder Bernini. During the summer visitors from all over the world come to drink its water, famous for its delicious sweet taste, and to recover a little before climbing the steps. The water also refreshes the blooms of the flowersellers who sit beneath great umbrellas at the foot of the steps and keep the square colorful whatever the season. And occasionally a young girl is sent by her mother to fill her pitcher with this special water.

The idle forms of resting travelers attract in particular those with nowhere to go, and many a Bohemian comes here and waits, as he does in Washington Square or Piccadilly Circus, for that elusive inspiration. The surrounding galleries and antique shops would have you believe that this is a second Greenwich Village, but the prices belie the fact and the authentic Italian artists have far less famous views from their garret windows. Caffè Greco, however, which has occupied the same site for two hundred years, was once the center of intellectual life.

The Spanish Steps, the steps of Trinità dei Monti, were built at the instigation of the French and made famous by the English who adopted the district two centuries ago. The English left at least one martyr to their beauty, for John Keats spent his last years in a house near the foot of the steps, and this was his final view of the world. Now climbing up the gradual slope, past the azaleas and the hippies selling trinkets, even the most mundane of us must feel he is on an aesthetic pilgrimage. And the reward at the top of the steps is the magnificent view out toward the Vatican.

Behind are the twin towers of the Church of Trinità dei Monti, built in 1495 long before the Steps were ever thought of. And behind the church are the Borghese Gardens which are reached by walking north along the Viale della Trinità dei Monti, and through the ramparts of Rome. It is good to come here during the heat of the late afternoon. The park belongs to the young and the young at heart. Children and dogs play on the grass and lovers get lost in the shrubberies or go for a row on the lake—with a backdrop of the Temple of Aesculapius. There is a feeling of carefully controlled wilderness, as though Nature understood that with such glorious surroundings she must be circumspect. The gardeners exercise their talents in the adjacent Pincio, designed 150 years ago; their flower beds are as precisely laid out as ever. And from here, on the Pincian Hill, surrounded by the silhouetted busts of famous Romans, are the most beautiful panoramas as the sun sets behind the dome of St. Peter's.

At the Corso, that sabre slash which cuts Renaissance Rome in two, is the Piazza del Popolo, the People's Square, an enormous example of neo-classical urban planning on a grand scale. It was designed by Valadier on the instructions of Napoleon. In the center is the Flaminian Obelisk, brought from Egypt in the days of the Empire. Some of its hieroglyphics refer to the glories of Ramases II who lived in the thirteenth century before Christ.

Occasionally between the Corso and the Tiber the tourist comes across streets that seem to attract less than their share of Rome's impatient traffic. Perhaps they were designed to discourage strangers by going nowhere in particular. In the middle of the twentieth century they have the opposite effect, for now they present a partial retreat from the constant turmoil that exists everywhere else in the city.

In the center of this district in the Piazza della Rotunda is that most majestic of Rome's ancient buildings, the Pantheon. It is probably the best-preserved remnant of Roman civilization and certainly the best in Rome. Erected in 27 B.C. and dedicated to Mars and Venus, it was rebuilt by Hadrian in A.D. 130 after a fire, and has remained standing to this day. It owes its survival to its consecration as a Christian church, which spared it from papal wrath. Even so it was occasionally plundered of its riches. Once it must have seemed like a golden mountain, but the gold plates which covered the roof were the first to go, followed by the precious marble and the bronze, sufficient for eighty cannon. The circular concrete dome is an amazing architectural feat. Its most characteristic feature is the hole in the center which is open to the elements, through which comes a shaft of dazzling sunlight to provide the only illumination. In the adjacent chapels are the tombs of some of the kings and queens of recent history, but it is the tomb of Raphael that receives the most frequent homage.

Although recently restored, in some contrast is the nearby Mausoleum of Augustus, the tomb of Augustus Caesar and his ancestors. Nearby, on the banks of the Tiber, surrounded by the wax images of his forefathers, the emperor's body was burned upon a pyre and, simultaneously, a caged eagle was released, symbolizing the soul freed to travel to the other side.

Our third journey starts on the Ponte S. Angelo above the

brown and sluggish Tiber, still meandering through history. We are welcomed by St. Peter and St. Paul who stand on the parapet accompanied by ten angels—"the breezy maniacs of Bernini"— forever combating an unseen storm. Enveloping the view on the right bank is the Castel S. Angelo, built by the Emperor Hadrian to house his remains and those of his heirs. Unfortunately he did not live to see it completed. Much of Rome's more violent history is associated with this castle; it is to this city what the Tower is to London.

Connected by a secret passage with the Vatican it became the alter ego of the Papacy. It was here that popes fled when their church was assailed. It got its name in 590 after Pope Gregory saw an angel sheathe his sword on the battlements, from which the Pope adjudged that the terrible plague then sweeping the city was ending. Later it was enlarged as a fortress with corner towers, gun platforms and barracks. And in 1527, during the sacking of Rome, Pope Clement VII took refuge here while the hordes of Germans and Spaniards turned St. Peter's into a stable. Later still it became a prison from which Benvenuto Cellini, the sculptor and adventurer, escaped and in which Beatrice Cenci, later to be romanticized by Shelley in *The Cenci*, was executed. Nowadays Castel S. Angelo is a museum.

Due west from this castle is St. Peter's. It is reached along the wide Via della Conciliazione built by Mussolini to replace a clutter of old streets which surrounded the Vatican. The Vatican City is a minute independent state under the sovereignty of the Pope. Prior to the unification of Italy the Pope had ruled the whole of Rome, but in 1879 he was deprived of his secular role and became "the prisoner of the Vatican." In 1929 the state of the Vatican City was created and its borders almost exactly coincide with the old medieval walls.

But it is more exhilarating to sidle up to St. Peter's more

obliquely, and enter St. Peter's Square through the Arch of Bells, past the watchful gaze of the Swiss Guard. The Square, the greatest architectural accomplishment of Bernini, is humbling. Its symmetry and harmony creates a feeling of solemnity which must impinge upon the soul of even the most frivolous tourist. On both sides of this elliptical "square" are long colonnades which support a roof adorned by 140 saints. These saints gaze out at the faithful who congregate on the cobbles below before moving off toward the steps of the cathedral.

Most of the superlatives of the Roman Catholic world are saved for the Basilica of St. Peter in the Vatican. Not only is it the largest, the most splendid, but, much more importantly, it is the most sacred building of the faith, and, in a sense, the oldest. The original basilica was built by Emperor Constantine in A.D. 319 on the site of the tomb of St. Peter. It was rebuilt a number of times, but the present structure was begun in A.D. 1506—and consecrated one hundred and twenty years later. A multitude of architects and artists helped in its creation, but it is Michelangelo who is most associated with its construction. Beneath the cupola he designed is an impression of enormous space. You enter expecting a sensation of confinement, only to find that every emotion flows from you in a glorious expanse. I am sure the sense of exhilaration which I am so conscious of is universal.

It is impossible here to attempt to describe all the sights and activities which overflow from the church. Let me just mention the bronze statue of the seated St. Peter whose foot has been stroked and kissed so often it is quite worn away. And of equal interest is the central altar, the Pope's Altar, where only he can say mass. Above is a great bronze canopy (the bronze, it is rumored, came from the Pantheon) and below is the Tomb of St. Peter. On either side are numerous other altars where visiting priests take turns saying the mass throughout the morning. Beneath the mosaic floor are the Vatican Grottoes, which contain the tombs of many popes. And beneath the crypt, intermingled with the foundations of the cathedral but visible through the gratings, are the tombs and relics of ancient Romans.

Behind the basilica is the Vatican Palace, a labyrinth of art and beauty which must be tackled, even by the enthusiastic, early and fresh. It is entered from the Viale Vaticano to the north. Probably your ultimate destination is the Sistine Chapel, but to reach it on the first day you must have considerable stamina—and blinkers.

Beauty is everywhere. But unlike more traditional museums, the setting itself is a delight: friezes, scrolls, cornices, everywhere you look there is something to exclaim about and examine. On, on, through endless corridors and halls. Faint-hearted tour groups return, the foot-weary falter by the wayside. But for those who endure this aesthetic ascent comes, at last, the Sistine Chapel.

And here, of all places, do not hurry. The lights are very low and for a while it is difficult to see very much—especially the frescoes on the high ceiling. The whole surface of the walls and ceilings is painted but all eyes strain to see the details of Michelangelo's Last Judgment behind the altar. The resplendent, musclebound Christ decrees eternal destiny.

27. The sunset is welcomed after a scorching Roman summer's day.

28. Roman farmers till their fields amid constant reminders of their ancestors and their achievements.

29. Cypresses and classical ruins line both sides of the ancient stone-paved Appian Way.

30–31. The baths of Caracalla, inaugurated in the year 217, were large enough to accommodate over fifteen hundred bathers at one time; on fine summer evenings now, the ruins are used for outdoor performances of opera.

◁ 32. Porta S. Paolo, in the Aurelian wall (*see previous page*), is named for St. Paul because the road that passes through it leads to the basilica consecrated to him.

33. Everywhere in Rome there are stray cats, but their favorite dwelling places are the lonely old ruins.

34. The Pyramid of Gaius Cestius, a sepulchral monument (*opposite*), is adjacent both to St. Paul's Gate and to the Protestant Cemetery, where Keats lies buried and where Trelawney interred Shelley's heart.

35. The Arch of Constantine, near the Colosseum, commemorates the famous victory at the Milvian Bridge; it was erected by the senate and people of Rome three years after the battle.

36. Interior (*overleaf*) of one of the world's most famous buildings, the Colosseum: it took nine years to build and could accommodate fifty thousand spectators.

37–39. Forum Romanum—the Roman Forum—was the first and the most famous of the city's forums; later forums were erected at imperial command. *Below*, the Arch of Titus, which commemorates the victory over the Jews and the sack of Jerusalem. *Right*, the lovely portico of the temple of Saturn. *Overleaf*, Trajan's market.

Life alla romana

On my first visit I had eaten frequently in restaurants and hotels, but on each occasion it was maddening to find the waiters did not understand my particular brand of English. The only way I could order was to point to the most succulent sounding consonants on the menu. But wherever I pointed I always seemed to be served the same tomato-cum-oregano-flavored spaghetti, good, only lacking in variety. On my second trip my horizons were widened, but it was not until my third visit that I could put myself confidently in the hands of the natives.

Wine, *vino*, is a must with every Italian meal. Surprisingly white wine, *vino bianco*, is preferred, and the most popular comes from the Frascati district and tastes delicious. Now, presented with a wine list in a strange restaurant I just say "*Vino bianco, Frascati.*" The waiter is impressed and the price is reasonable. In my opinion only a fool would order French wine in Rome. And the people put on no airs when it comes to choosing the "right" wine to suit the meal. They pour it into unassuming glasses and toss it down in one gulp. The most famous red wine is the *vino rosso* produced in the Tuscany region and the Chianti which also comes from there. Each restaurant has its particular house wine (*vino della casa*) which is cheap and tastes good.

On that first evening after I had been welcomed into the house of my new artist friend, he took me out to a local restaurant. I still remember the meal well. The first thing to appear on the table was the wine, well cooled and finely flavored. It seems to cascade through the body, settling the dust and soothing the aches of the day. Looking out across the square, I felt for a moment that the wine was a small reflection of the fountain there, constantly cooling and refreshing the surrounding air.

For hors d'oeuvres, or antipasto, we had figs and cured ham (*prosciutto e fichi*), which together with melon and ham are the most popular hors d'oeuvres in Rome. Eaten with sticks of bread called *grissini*, they are excellent.

The next dish we were served was *spaghetti alle vongole*, which is spaghetti served with a clam sauce. And this was followed by grilled shrimp, *scampi alla griglia*. Lemon juice is sprinkled over the shrimp before eating. And what a delicious dish it is! Italy abounds with seafood—lobsters, shrimps, and shellfish. After thousands of years the Mediterranean still gives a fair harvest, though now much of the fish has to come from further afield.

For dessert we had huge platefuls of Italian ice cream that I had heard so much about but never had the courage to ask for. And over thick black coffee, our two-hour meal wound slowly to a close. Although they eat quickly, Italians spend hours on their meals. Everyone is always laughing and shouting, creating a convivial atmosphere quite unlike a typical Japanese meal. The waiters, too, are a cheery crew, even if some of them seem intent on abducting the ladies in your party. And singers, in groups or individually, make their way round the tables singing *canzoni* with varying expertise and gypsy songs.

Why Italians should have developed such gargantuan appetites I cannot understand. With bib tucked into collar, wineglass in one hand and spaghetti fork in the other those swarthy tanned young men and svelte girls seem to visibly expand behind their napkins. At the end of meal upon meal all is lost to a uniform roundness in man and woman alike. Of course I exaggerate, but it seems a pity. The *pasta* is the worst culprit. Meat is not especially popular among Romans, certainly not in large quantities. Caesar commented in his memoirs that his men were complaining and getting listless after a diet of animal meat and no grain.

The usual custom in Rome is a heavy meal in the middle of the day. After a light breakfast, most people start work early, often before sunrise. Then everyone tries to get home in time for the 1 P.M. TV news which must be the most popular program in the country. Afterward comes a two-hour lunch during which the local politicians and sportsmen are variously praised and cursed with such enthusiasm that a two-hour siesta is essential—though it is rumored that this is when most Romans are fathered. Somewhere between four and five in the afternoon the shops and offices open again, and the poor tourist who half an hour ago had begun to think the citizens had deserted him is swamped by the third traffic jam of the day. Then suddenly it is time to eat again, and as lavishly as one can afford; the restaurants again become the focal points of the energy and bustle of the city.

For the visitor the best food is rarely found in hotels. The *ristoranti* are the high-class restaurants, the *trattorie* and *hosterie* usually serve more modest fare, while the *pizzerie* are popular for a light meal. But *ristoranti*, although they almost invariably have the highest prices, do not always serve the best food. The *trattorie* have a better reputation, but it is the Hostaria dell'Orso which is often claimed to be the best restaurant and it is here that I used to take some of the more important people I was obliged to entertain. I took my friends to less elegant places where the atmosphere was more congenial and I, personally, feel the food is better. For example, those in the Trastevere (such as Sabatini) are filled with *bonhomie*, though few foreigners went there until recently. Any taxi driver can take you there. Actually there are three restaurants run by three brothers. There used to be only one but it was so successful that they all became independent and set up in friendly rivalry. *Spaghetti alle vongole* is one of the specialities of the house. Sitting out in summer under the stars, the Gods and Goddesses of Rome, immersing myself in the charm and music of Italy, I am convinced that Rome is still the center of the civilized world.

It seems that half of what gets done in Rome is accomplished around the hour of twilight. It is as if the whole day was just a build-up to this evening climax. Deals are struck, old friends are met and new ones found, appointments are made and kept, marriages made and broken. Only the visitor has time on his hands, wondering what to do before dinner, perhaps wasting it in some hotel room with tired feet and dressing for a staid, irrelevant meal, or sitting perplexed in a sidewalk cafe as all of life is erupting around him, and he watches the fringed umbrellas come down.

And now two hours later, satiated and relaxed, you are alone with your companion and the lights of Rome. Spotlights shine on the Colosseum and pick up the arches in the Roman Forum. Hidden colored lights illuminate the fountains so the water drips from the carvings like liquid gold. On summer nights music from the outdoor concerts drifts over the traffic to the tops of Rome's hills—both man's and Nature's.

Then one last fling and then another one in the bars and nightclubs of the Via Veneto and its shady back alleys. A few tips for the cost-conscious: sit at the bar, pay for a round of drinks as you get them, and remember the hostesses seem to have an expensive penchant for champagne.

Surprisingly little of the Roman diet is imported. They have never had cause to be dissatisfied with their menu, so they have never chosen to change it. Much of the shopping is still done at traditional markets with the sellers glorifying and the housewives disparaging the produce. It is a perfect opportunity for nonmalicious argument—a skill at which all excel and enjoy practicing. Supermarkets must be destroying the soul of the Roman housewife. The whole concept of a fixed price is anathema to them.

Because of the reliance on indigenous produce, the food available changes with the seasons. Fruit is always popular, but especially in summer when the farmers and their offspring settle with their crop on every street corner and market alley. Piles of watermelons are trundled into the city each morning on dilapidated trucks. Children on bicycles chase them along rough cobbled streets waiting for one to bounce off. In September the stores are full of mushrooms of startling shapes and colors: speckled green or flaring crimson, they lie in shop windows like so many dormant monsters waiting for a victim.

Fish have a weekly cycle. The freshest are on Tuesday and Friday. Fishmongers, who are a race apart since the business has gone from father to son for hundreds of years, come into their own each Friday morning when the lines are longest, the audience is biggest, and the buyers a captive market.

Perhaps because the act of purchasing is still such a battle of wits, shopping is never considered a chore in Rome. Whether one is trying on the latest bizarre fashions along the Via Condotti (where lately the men outnumber the women), or in some small alley arguing across a makeshift stall, the essence of the transaction is the same. The bargains are off in some distant corner of the town where it is more important to be well versed in the gestures of Italy than it is to know the spoken language. Hands spread-eagled across the heart and eyes cast heavenward mean "Signor, you must be crazy. My children will starve, my wife will leave me." The fingers brought together before the mouth formed for a kiss mean "This is the very best Italian silk made from hand-picked worms fed off an ancient mulberry tree." And before each bargain is made there is a great sigh from the vendor at the prospect of the ruin that faces him. But someone has always bought one cheaper. When in Rome, however hard you try, you can never quite do as the Romans do.

Appearances are everything. The impeccable dandy, confident as he gazes haughtily at a ravishing beauty, is a clerk in a grocery store enjoying his day off. He spent half an hour pressing his only pair of trousers that morning, as he does every morning. He sleeps with his hair in a hairnet. He disdains the flamboyant fashions of the foreigner—only his cufflinks and handkerchief are flashes of color. He looks beautiful and he loves it. The world is his prey.

Back home, in a six-story walk-up apartment house, in the company of the only people who really matter in his life, he carefully removes and neatly puts away his outer shell and relaxes in overalls and underwear. The Italian man is still very much the master of his household. Divorce, although recently legalized, is still looked on with horror and shame. Whether a woman marries for love, family honor or a rich son-in-law for her parents, she is supposed to marry for life. The husband holds the purse strings and his wife does the housework. Even if she has her own job she is still expected to prepare all the meals and keep the children under control.

In his spare time the man's chief preoccupation seems to be politics. Despite two world wars and the growth of communism, the Romans' chief loyalties are based on geography. Two quite different races find an uneasy coexistence in the capital. The Roman by temperament favors the southerners, who consider the northerners upstarts and not genuine Italians, but he is conscious of the barbs that the northerners throw at those who lack their technical skills and he is careful not to overidentify.

Milan is already the center of industry and much of the commerce. In today's European Common Market a more logical capital would be in the north near the factories and the associate countries. History and the power of the Church keeps the capital in Rome and no Roman is going to allow it to move.

These bipartisan feelings come most to the fore at football matches. There is only one sport in Rome: soccer. The stars of the field outshine those of the political rostrum and celluloid screen (with the single exception of Sophia Loren, who is almost a living goddess to the poor and downtrodden.) Newspapers eulogize their talents and woe betide any foreign team that wins on Italian soil. Important matches are heralded for days on end by the press who can find little else to comment on. The day of the match might resemble a day at the games of ancient Rome. Crowds fill the streets waving flags and chanting the names of their heroes. If the match is between a northern and a southern team, tempers are especially high, for honor is at stake. The impassioned arguments that are the bread and butter of most Italian conversation usually fade quickly and apparent enemies are soon friends again, but arguments about the superior qualities of respective provinces can never be forgotten—and only soccer heroes can properly avenge a slight.

While the men devote themselves to politics and soccer, many women seem to find solace in the Church. No town could possibly have more churches, and yet even in these times which have seen the rapid increase of religious apathy in many countries, Rome's churches are often as not quite full, be they great seventeeth-century cathedrals or small neighborhood chapels. Most men who visit go early in the morning on their way to the office or factory, and this is the most popular time for women, too. Even so, many come back later, before lunch, when there is more time to pray and contemplate. The Catholic faith offers much, but in return demands much too.

The characteristic of the Romans which is at once both their most charming and most infuriating quality can be summed up in the word *accidenti*. Meaning something like "Bad luck!", it is a sympathetic gesture of commiseration in the face of trying circumstances or outright misfortune, and yet uttering it strips the speaker of any responsibility for those circumstances or that misfortune, laying the blame squarely on the way things are, on "life," on fate.

Thus if you are stomping restlessly up and down the lobby of your hotel as the time of your train, always prompt since Mussolini's reform, comes and goes, the only involvement the proprietor will express in the situation is "*Accidenti!*"—"So sorry!"—though he knows full well that the driver of the hotel bus is fast asleep upstairs after a too-liquid lunch. If you attempt to cross the road at a pedestrian crossing, making a desperate lunge for your life at the last moment as a car brushes your coat and charges on, the chances are that the driver never noticed you at all; but he just might turn around with a smile and the word "*Accidenti!*" on his lips.

It is possible to live in Rome and never get used to this exasperating philosophy. But to survive a prolonged stay in the city there is another aspect of the local temperament to which it is essential to become accustomed. I refer to time. Time is now. Or more exactly, time is today, tomorrow, and "I'll call you." Whatever one wants to do, one should be doing at that particular moment. So why make detailed arrangements for the future? The future has always managed before and will look after itself. Live for today. With over two thousand years of history behind them, and all around them a history in which Rome and her citizens were never far from the forefront, they, of all people, should know.

40. Fresh vegetables and fruit abound in Roman marketplaces. When in season, they are—or used to be—quite cheap.

41–45. The city's large food markets offer just about everything the housewife may want. Shown on this page are fish, snails and the fruit of the prickly pear cactus; *opposite*, poultry stalls. *Overleaf*, birds for eating and birds for listening to and looking at share the same market.

46–49. Food in Rome is excellent and varied: artichokes (*right*) are often served as an antipasto; favorites for an entrée are grilled prawns (*below*) and grilled meat (*opposite*). *Below right*, a *salumera*, with its collection of sausages and cheeses.

50–56. Wine and music: both are essential accompaniments to a happy Roman meal, and the music is as varied as the wine. *Opposite*, a bamboo flute from Sicily, a vibraphone, a tambourine, and an accordion. *Overleaf*, a complete—and vivacious—ensemble.

57–63. Roman faces are the most expressive in the world, and no one in their right mind ever objects to posing for a picture.

65. At the Sunday morning flea-market near Porta Portese (*right*), the wary shopper may find occasional bargains—provided he is willing to haggle.

64. An outdoor exhibition of the works of promising young painters is held each year in Via Margutta, Rome's "Latin Quarter."

66. The gardens of the Villa Borghese, central Rome's chief and most popular park, are English rather than Italian in style.

67. Autumn in Rome—the famous *ottobrata romana* —is considered by both Romans and visitors alike to be the best time of year in the Eternal City.

◁ 68. A grandmother (*see previous page*) poses cheerfully for her picture at her seventy-eighth birthday party.

69–71. Grapes for wine are grown in almost every part of Italy, from Piedmont to Sicily, and the Roman countryside is no exception. The wines produced there are called Castelli Romani; they may be either white or red and they include such familiar vintages as Frascati, Albano and Montefiascone.

72–74. At the wine festival of Marino in the Roman countryside, townsfolk garb themselves in antique costumes and spend the days and the nights of the festival (which takes place in early October) singing and dancing and parading through the streets, eating and—of course—drinking.

THIS BEAUTIFUL WORLD

- The Himalayas
- Palaces of Kyoto
- Peking
- Gods of Kumano
- Moscow
- Michelangelo
- Afghanistan
- Hawaii
- Seoul
- Goya
- The Alps
- The Acropolis
- Vienna
- African Animals
- Thailand
- Yosemite
- San Francisco
- Bali
- Spain
- Mexico
- Imperial Villas of Kyoto
- Journey through Africa
- The Grand Canyon
- California
- Mongolia
- Lapland
- The Greek Islands
- Hong Kong
- Angkor Wat
- Istanbul
- The Road to Holy Mecca
- Burma
- The Andes
- New Guinea
- Marketplaces of the World
- Tokyo
- Ireland
- Australia
- India
- Cherry Blossoms
- Okinawa
- New York
- London
- Sri Lanka
- Iran
- Yugoslavia
- Washington
- Rome
- Brazil

In preparation

- Alaska
- Dehli